Original title:
Timber Tattles

Copyright © 2025 Creative Arts Management OÜ
All rights reserved.

Author: Adrian Caldwell
ISBN HARDBACK: 978-1-80567-426-9
ISBN PAPERBACK: 978-1-80567-725-3

Parables of Pine

In the forest, secrets roam,
Pine cones gossip, call it home.
Squirrels crack jokes, oh what fun,
While birds chirp tunes under the sun.

Trees sway gently, sharing a laugh,
Roots entangle in a silly path.
Evergreen eyes catch a friendly glance,
Nature's party, come join the dance!

Beneath the Boughs

Under branches, tales take flight,
Frogs in tuxedos, what a sight!
Crickets play cards, night brings a cheer,
A raccoon's laughter rings loud and clear.

The woodpecker's drumming brings forth a beat,
As chipmunks prepare for a dance-off meet.
All while the owls hoot wise refrain,
"Mischief is best when it doesn't cause pain!"

The Whispered Wisdom

Leaves rustle softly, secrets unfurl,
Bees buzzing gossip like a whirl.
Mice in the bushes collaborating,
Storytime laughter, no hesitating.

A wise old owl starts the show,
"Who's got the best tale? Let's go!"
Each creature shares with a chuckle and grin,
In the forest theatre, all feel like kin.

Legends of the Leaf

Once a leaf claimed to be the best,
Said to its friends, "You'll never guess!"
Dancing with breeze, singing its song,
But fell off the branch; what went wrong?

Fungi chuckled, "You can't be grand!"
While critters took turns to understand.
With laughter in circles, they spun a new tale,
Leaving behind a leaf in the vale!

Embers of the Evergreen

In a forest, where whispers thrive,
The squirrels dance, oh so alive.
A beaver wore his finest hat,
While raccoons laughed and shared a chat.

The owls hooted with great flair,
As rabbits pranced without a care.
Branches tickled the sky's blue cheek,
Nature's secrets made them leak.

A pinecone rolled, it made a scene,
All critters laughed, it wiped them clean.
With every crackle and pop, they cheer,
Those tales of wood echoed far and near.

Pondering Pines

Tall pines ponder in the sun,
Debating if they've had their fun.
"Should we sway or stay so still?"
"Let's see who feels the strongest thrill!"

A squirrel shouted, "You're too slow!"
"Let's race the winds, come on, let's go!"
Branches stretched and roots did shake,
While grumpy old stones began to quake.

With a whoosh, the leaves did fly,
One shouted, "Look, I'm soaring high!"
The others giggled in their place,
As pine needles danced a silly race.

The Canopy's Clamor

Up high where the canopy meets the sprite,
The twigs pretend to have some height.
"Watch me jump!" the branches cried,
While the dandelions laughed and snide.

The birds squawked tunes that made no sense,
While butterflies twirled, a magical dance.
The sun peeked through, a shy little face,
With beams of light, they joined the chase.

The chitter-chatter echoed wide,
Underneath, the small critters tried to hide.
It's a ruckus of joy, pure delight,
As the forest giggles into the night.

Sentinels of the Sky

Tall sentinels stand side by side,
With branches that sweep and glide.
They made a pact to tell a tale,
Of every wind, storm, and hail.

"Remember when we were just small seeds?"
They chuckled at their humble needs.
"Now look at us, so grand and bold,"
Their stories worth more than gold.

The clouds played tricks, as they spun fast,
Creating shadows that never last.
With every gust, they shared a laugh,
While nature penned its own photograph.

Fragmented Fronds

In a forest where ferns play,
Jumping jigs in the bright day.
With each wave, they sway so fine,
"Look at me! I'm a plant, divine!"

Squirrels giggle, watching them dance,
As leaves flutter in a leafy trance.
"Who knew grass could be such fun?
There's no party like a plant one!"

The Poetry of the Falling Leaves

A leaf dropped down with a little twirl,
"Check me out! I'm quite the girl!"
Spinning, twirling, proclaiming joy,
"A little dance, oh boy, oh boy!"

The ground's a canvas of colors bright,
Leaves chat gossip from morning to night.
"Did you see? That one just flew by!
Next week, I think it's my time to fly!"

Bark and Branches: A Saga

The branches huddled in jabbering trees,
"Who's got the funniest stories, please?"
Bark-chewing insects adorned their rings,
"Tell us tales, oh wise old things!"

One said, "Once I kissed a wise old crow,
But he stole my acorns, a real low blow!"
Laughter echoed through the green canopy,
"Let's do it again, such fun with glee!"

The Language of the Lichen

Two lichens sat on a rock so grand,
Talking secrets, not quite planned.
"Did you hear about the moss next door?
He thinks he's too cool, but he's quite a bore!"

With each chuckle, the sun held its gaze,
As they shared silly tales of their days.
"Let's make a banner, say 'moss is a pest'
And have a lichen party—oh, that sounds the best!"

Rustling Leaves

In the breeze, they dance and swirl,
Whispers shared, secrets unfurl.
Squirrels gossip with cheeky pleas,
Judging the acorns with laughter and wheeze.

Rabbits hop with tales so grand,
While crickets play in a mischievous band.
Each rustle hides a silly truth,
Nature's vibe with a hint of sleuth.

Hidden Truths

Beneath the boughs, laughter spills,
Critters concocting their funny thrills.
A raccoon's prank, a squirrel's jest,
Who can resist a frolicsome fest?

Amid the roots, secrets play,
Old logs echo a foolish ballet.
Nature's jesters, with one twin goal,
To spin us tales while losing control.

The Canopy's Confessions

In the leaves, the gossip flows,
Chirping tales the canopy knows.
A wise old owl hoots a ticklish pun,
While branches shake from laughter begun.

Breezes stir with a giggly tone,
As sunlight filters through, overgrown.
Every rustle is a joke in disguise,
A playful world under wide-open skies.

Bark-etched Stories

Carved in bark, the scribbles tease,
Adventures chronicled in the trees.
A heart entwined with a squirrel's name,
The woods remember, though they feel no shame.

Fungi giggle at every turn,
Mushroom caps nod as critters yearn.
These ancient stories bring laughter in waves,
Echoing through the woodland caves.

Shadows of the Forest Floor

In the shadows, mischief brews,
Mice in huddles share their views.
A pinecone rolls, a hidden seed,
Spreading laughter with glee and speed.

The underbrush hums a silly rhyme,
As fireflies dance to the rhythm of time.
In every nook, a jest is found,
Nature's humor surrounds the ground.

The Narrative of Nature

In the heart of the woods, a squirrel took flight,
Chasing a dream that turned into fright.
He leaped from a branch with a wobble and squeak,
Landing on pine cones that made him quite weak.

The owls had a meeting, all hooting with glee,
Watching the antics of this bold bumblebee.
He buzzed 'round the trees like a small, dizzy kite,
While branches all whispered, 'What a comical sight!'

Then came a raccoon with a plan in his head,
To steal every acorn from underneath beds.
But the wise old crows saw this mischief unfold,
And cawed out loud, 'This fool's getting bold!'

The trees all chuckled, their leaves shaking bright,
As creatures played games, dancing under moonlight.
Nature's own circus, a quirky delight,
In the forest of folly, everything's right!

The Arborist's Chronicle

An arborist climbed with a belt and a saw,
Swinging through branches without a flaw.
But he tripped on a root, tumbled down with a thud,
Covered in leaves and a big, muddy stud.

The birds gathered round, chirping in fits,
Watching the scene with their beaky skits.
The branches all jiggled, they twirled with the breeze,
While the man in the mud yelled, 'What a great tease!'

A snail wobbled by, it turned to the crowd,
Said, 'Moving too fast? You should try slow and proud!'
The laughter erupted, echoing through the air,
As creatures joined in, with nary a care.

With a chuckle and grin, he stood up at last,
Brushed off the dirt and embraced every blast.
The forest was lively, alive with its quirks,
Noticing that nature can sometimes be jerks!

Confessions of Canopies

Once I was an oak, quite sturdy and tall,
But I harbored a secret, preparing to fall.
The winds they were gossiping, swirling about,
They whispered my fate, causing me doubt.

Then came a chipmunk, with a grin that was sly,
'Tell me your worries, don't be shy!'
I shared my woes, feeling quite low,
And he laughed so hard, he fell in the snow.

'Fear not,' squeaked the chipmunk, 'it's just a bad breeze,

We all have our moments of fumbling with trees.'
The leaves were all nodding, in sympathy sweet,
A canopy meeting, such a funny retreat!

Now I sway with the gusts, no longer a fright,
Embracing my quirks under stars shining bright.
In this whimsical grove, we dance in the light,
Swaying with laughter, taking wrongs to delight.

The Sylvan Stories

Deep in the forest, where stories unfold,
A fox found a hat that was shiny and bold.
He pranced like a prince, with a flair, oh so grand,
While mockingbird chirped, 'What's the plan, woodland band?'

Then came a deer with a head full of dreams,
Said, 'Let's throw a party, or so it seems!'
The trees shook with laughter, all rustling their leaves,
As the critters conspired, plotting fun eves.

A rabbit brought snacks, and a porcupine too,
With quills all a-jangle, he hailed the crew.
The dance floor emerged, made entirely of sprigs,
While shadows of squirrels did whimsical gigs.

At the end of the night, as dawn painted gold,
The forest decided they'd be brave and bold.
With laughter still ringing, they vowed to repeat,
The joy of this night—a whimsical treat!

Shadows of the Silent Grove

In the hush of the night, they giggle and sigh,
Whispers of leaves in a fluttering fly.
Squirrels exchange tales of their acorn stash,
While owls hoot loudly, a feathery clash.

Rabbits are plotting, oh what a riot,
Drawing up schemes, like a tree-based diet.
With branches as arms, they'd dance in delight,
Who knew that the woods could be such a sight?

A raccoon reveals his latest disguise,
While chipmunks roll eyes, making fun of his size.
The shadows are filled with laughter and jest,
Nature's own theater, who could've guessed?

So chuckle along as the branches sway low,
Each twig has a story from high to below.
In whispered confessions beneath the full moon,
The forest keeps secrets, and always makes room.

The Grove's Gentle Gossip

In the heart of the grove, under branches so wide,
The flowers are gossiping, blooming with pride.
With petals a-quiver, they whisper and tease,
About all the creatures who dart through the trees.

The frogs croak a tune, their rhythm's a charm,
As ants march in line, with a lunchbox of harm.
The bees buzz around with a sweet little prank,
Making fun of the snail with his slow-moving flank.

A butterfly flutters, quick with a quip,
Telling tales of the caterpillar's latest trip.
With laughter like raindrops, the gossip takes flight,
As day turns to dusk, and the stars shine so bright.

But beware of the owl, with his wise, watchful eye,
He'll shush the whole grove with a knowing reply.
For stories may linger in whispers of green,
In the grove where the laughter is always serene.

Bark and Bough

The trees lean in close, sharing secrets anew,
With bark that can talk, and a canopy too.
A funny old oak laughs at the pine's silly hat,
While birch rolls her eyes, saying, "Look at that!"

The willow gives hugs, with her long, dangling hair,
As squirrels spin tales without any care.
The branches all sway like they're part of a show,
As shadows unite in the soft evening glow.

A crow caws loudly, claiming all the best spots,
While the sparrows throw pebbles and gather the knots.
Every twig has a tale of the sights that they've seen,
From the ups and the downs of the forest routine.

So when you're feeling down, just glance at the trees,
Their laughter will lift you, like a gentle breeze.
For in every bough, and every old bark,
There's a spark of joy hidden deep in the dark.

Confessions of the Copse

In a little old copse, where whispers resound,
The bushes exchange tales, all funny and round.
With thorns and soft petals, they swap little pranks,
As mushrooms stand guard, with their quirky little ranks.

A doe munches quietly, but hears the good joke,
About a lost hedgehog who rolled past a smoke.
The trees shake with laughter, their leaves all a-quiver,
As the brook adds its voice, making the moment deliver.

The robins debate who can sing the most high,
While the shy little mouse swears she's always nearby.
Amidst all the chatter, one peep softly chimes,
"Why can't we all dance? We've got boughs for our rhymes!"

So join in the fun, and don't be so serious,
For laughter in nature can be quite delirious.
In the copse where they gather, each story's a gem,
Full of giggles and grins, the forest's own whim.

Confessions of the Canopy

Leaves gossip loudly in the breeze,
Squirrels holding court with ease.
Branchy banter fills the air,
Woodpecker tales without a care.

Raccoons plotting midnight feasts,
While owls hoot jokes to say the least.
Vines entwined like tangled hair,
Nature's giggles everywhere.

Acorns tumble, roll, and bounce,
While rabbits hop and chase and pounce.
Mice steal seeds with little stealth,
Funny thieves enhancing health.

In this leafy world so bright,
Every day brings pure delight.
With laughter swirling all around,
Joyful secrets can be found.

Whispers in the Woods

The pine trees murmur with a cheer,
Windy whispers only they can hear.
Frogs croak jokes as crickets laugh,
Echoes dance on nature's path.

Bunnies wear their silliest hats,
While squirrels jest about their spats.
Each twig snaps with playful grace,
Creating mischief in this place.

Owls wink with a knowing glance,
As fireflies light up the night's dance.
Mushrooms giggle, rocking so slow,
Underneath, the critters glow.

In this forest, filled with fun,
Every creature's on the run.
Whispered secrets, oh so sly,
Nature's laughter, soaring high.

Secrets of the Sapling

A little sprout stands proud and tall,
With stories just waiting for the call.
Tiny roots tangle underground,
Searching for laughter all around.

Nearby, a hedgehog wears a crown,
Trading jokes like a furry clown.
The sun nods down with a bright smile,
As bees buzz by all the while.

Butterflies flutter, striking poses,
While dandelions blow like roses.
Saplings giggle at the sight,
Sharing secrets, taking flight.

In the garden where they thrive,
Only the brave and bold arrive.
They whisper tales of days gone by,
With every breeze that passes by.

Echoes of the Evergreen

Evergreens chuckle, standing proud,
While secrets bubble up, aloud.
A deer jokes softly with a hare,
Their laughter echoes everywhere.

Moonlit nights and shadows play,
With owls sharing stories that sway.
Spruces sway, keeping abeat,
Their branches tapping, oh so sweet.

Mossy humor delights the ground,
With every rustle, joy is found.
Sunlight twinkles through the leaves,
As nature's laughter never weaves.

In this realm of green and gold,
The funniest tales of life unfold.
Rustling whispers create delight,
In the heart of the starry night.

Echoes of the Elder

In the forest, whispers play,
Old oaks have tales, all day.
Squirrels gossip, branches sway,
Every twig has something to say.

A pine tree chuckles, thick with glee,
"I've seen more than you, wait and see!"
Jokes cascade like leaves in fall,
Nature's humor tickles all.

The maples giggle, their colors bright,
"Turn up the sap and get it right!"
Bark to bark, each word a jest,
In this woods, they never rest.

Listen close, the stories bloom,
From roots below to leafy room.
Laughs echo through the green terrain,
In the grove, humor reigns.

The Nectar of Narrative

Sweet tales drip from every leaf,
Bees buzz stories, oh so brief.
A robin chirps in rhythmic quips,
While blossoms giggle with their lips.

"Did you hear what that tree said?"
A buzzing bee, no need for dread.
Pollen parties in the air,
Nature's jokes beyond compare.

The flowers wink and nod their heads,
Whispering dreams where laughter spreads.
"Come gather round the shady glen,
The best tales come from roots and men!"

Jokes pour sweet like honey's flow,
Each petal's chuckle, softly low.
With every breeze, a new delight,
The stories dance until the night.

Grove Gatherings

Underneath the leafy spread,
Squirrels gather, tales to thread.
"Did you hear, the pines can dance?"
All their chatter sets the chance.

The bushes giggle, wagging leaves,
"Last summer's tales give us reprieves!"
Branches bounce with playful jest,
Humor fills the wild fest.

A curious crow with jokes to tell,
Perches high, creating a spell.
"Why did the tree stand so tall?
To hear the best gossip of all!"

And so they laugh, the grove alive,
With stories swirling, hearts arrive.
In every rustle, giggles bloom,
Nature's humor fills the room.

The Story in the Sap

Sap drips down, sticky and sweet,
Each drop whispers, can't be beat.
Telling tales of sun and rain,
Of squirrels scurrying, not a strain.

"Hey there, buddy, what's your plan?"
"Just sipping nectar, like a fan!"
In the slow glow of afternoon,
Nature cracks up, a funny tune.

Beneath thick bark, secrets lay,
Woodpeckers knock and join the fray.
"Knock, knock! Who's there? A tree!"
With laughter, they dance with glee.

So gather round, come take a sip,
The stories flow from every drip.
In every groove, a chuckle waits,
Nature's humor resonates.

The Sylvan Saga

In the woods where whispers play,
Trees chime in a funny way.
Bark to bark, they share a peek,
Of squirrel antics, oh so cheek!

The owl hoots with a knowing grin,
While rabbits roll, they laugh and spin.
A bear strolls by, looking quite spry,
But even he can't tell a lie!

Branches sway with every jest,
As chipmunks gather, trying their best.
Leaves titter at every surprise,
Nature's jesters with twinkling eyes!

At sunset's glow, the giggles rise,
Echoing tales of woodland fries.
In this grove of laughter free,
Every creature plays the comedy!

Gossip Among the Green

Among the leaves where secrets swirl,
The vines and ferns begin to twirl.
Laughter bubbles from roots below,
As gossipy winds begin to blow!

The crows caw tales that twist and twine,
Of owls who think they look divine.
Grasshoppers leap in playful cheer,
Chirping truths both far and near!

A woodpecker knocks with a funny beat,
While hedgehogs huddle with nimble feet.
Every critter adds their tease,
In this forest, it's a breeze!

The whispers rise from dusk till dawn,
Of acorns tossed and laughter drawn.
In this green realm, no woes are seen,
Just tales that stir between the green!

The Aspens' Arrangement

In a grove of aspens, tall and bright,
Leaves shimmy under the sun's warm light.
They gossip sweetly, all in a row,
About the tales of seeds that glow!

Two squirrels dance, their tails in a twirl,
While ants in line do a little whirl.
'Did you hear about that nutty bloom?'
The trees shake with laughter; there's plenty of room!

The breeze tickles with a playful tease,
As whispers whisper 'Oh, please, oh please!'
Branches sway like they know the score,
These merry aspens never bore!

At twilight's call, their voices blend,
As nature laughs, and hearts extend.
In this aspen haven where fun ignites,
The stories thrive on moonlit nights!

The Sapwood's Story

In the heart of the tree, the sapwood laughs,
Sharing stories of nature's calks and drafts.
A beaver shares tales of busy days,
While the mushrooms giggle in sunny rays!

The birdies chirp with jubilant glee,
A contest of who can swing from the tree.
Even the slugs sing a tune so slow,
Proclaiming their secrets, oh, don't you know?

The wind joins in, giving all a spin,
As everything sways, let the fun begin!
Snapping twigs clap like an audience cheer,
For every tall tale told, they want to hear!

In the hub of the wood, where stories entangle,
Beneath the bark, the chuckles dangle.
Life's a comedy in every nook,
In the sapwood's embrace, come take a look!

Nature's Veiled Testimonies

In the woods where whispers roam,
The trees gossip, a leafy dome.
Squirrels tattle with cheeky pride,
As they scurry, the secrets they hide.

Rabbits share tales of their wild leaps,
While owls hoot, their knowledge deep.
A breeze carries laughter all around,
Nature's own tales, profound yet sound.

Beneath the Foliage: A Tale

Underneath the leafy crown,
A critter circus leaps and bounds.
Frogs croak jokes in a ribbit rhyme,
Each punchline hits just in time.

Ladybugs roll their tiny eyes,
As the ants march in silly guise.
Nature's jesters, all in a row,
Beneath the green, the laughter flows.

Stories in the Splinters

In the log where woodpeckers play,
Splinters hold stories, come what may.
Beetles boast of their mighty might,
While spiders spin tales late at night.

The old tree groans, a wise old sage,
Whispering secrets from a bygone age.
Branches sway in a giggling dance,
Each shake revealing a humorous chance.

The Earth's Confidants

The rocks chuckle, ancient and bold,
Sharing secrets quietly told.
With every crack, a story unfolds,
Of woodland adventures in days of old.

The flowers blush with vibrant hues,
While bees buzz softly, sharing clues.
Beneath the sky, they gather in glee,
The Earth's whispers, wild and free.

Secrets in the Shadows

In the woods where whispers play,
Trees tell tales in a funny way.
Squirrels speak of acorn gold,
While leaves gossip, brave and bold.

A pine tree dressed in a silly hat,
Claims he saw a dancing cat.
Branches shake with laughter loud,
As the forest holds a chuckling crowd.

Mossy floors are stage and scene,
For rabbits in their silly sheen.
They pirouette, they leap and bound,
While the roots chuckle at the sound.

In the shadows, secrets hide,
Each crack of bark, a tale implied.
Nature's muse brings laughs to sprout,
In the forest, joy flows out.

Reveries of the Redwoods

High above, the redwoods jest,
As critters cause a merry fest.
Owls hoot songs of olden days,
While branches sway in breezy plays.

A woodpecker with painted nails,
Tells of shipwrecks and laughing whales.
The sun peeks through in golden beams,
While shadows dance in funny dreams.

Frogs in coats of leafy green,
Waltz along the forest scene.
Whispers echo in playful tunes,
As the woodlands sway beneath the moons.

Even the stumps seem to grin,
In this world where fun begins.
Every rustle and crack of bark,
Makes nature's laughter light the dark.

The Dialogue of the Dense

Among the thickets, chatter's rife,
Branches tease about their life.
Bumblebees in bowties hum,
While flowers roll, and giggle, and strum.

The bushes gossip, full of mirth,
Who's the fairest of the earth?
A little lizard, sly and spry,
Claims the sun is just a pie.

Vines entwined in playful slips,
Swaying to the chatter's quips.
A deer jumps in, with playful grace,
As laughter echoes through the space.

In every nook, a tale unfolds,
Nature's laughter never old.
With each rustle, beams of glee,
In the dense, fun's the key.

Saga of the Sequoia

Sequoias boast of ancient lore,
With every ring, they want to score.
A raccoon clad in fancy threads,
Narrates tales that twist our heads.

The trickster fox peeks from the green,
Says the world's a crazy scene!
Chirping crickets join the play,
Adding rhythms to their sway.

High above, a bird doth sing,
Of nutty dreams and joyful flings.
With merry chirps and cheeky caws,
They serenade with nature's applause.

In the heart of life's grand show,
Sequoias watch the fun flow.
Each chuckle, each laugh, a joyous mark,
As the forest ignites a spark.

The Tales Trees Tell

In the woods, a maple danced,
Laughing leaves, their prance enhanced.
Squirrels giggled at the show,
Twisting branches, don't you know?

Once a pine had quite a scare,
A raccoon climbed to style its hair.
But upside down, it lost its grip,
Fell in a heap—what a funny trip!

Birch trees whisper silly jokes,
While the oaks just roll their folks.
Nature's humor, wild and free,
The forest's laugh is pure glee!

So next time you hear a creak,
Know a tree has jokes to speak.
In the shade, feel the bright jest,
For the woods are laughing at their best!

Fables of the Forest Floor

Fungi gather, telling tales,
Under leaves, the laughter sails.
Chipmunks chirp with fruity cheer,
Spreading gumdrops, never fear!

A hedgehog wore a knitty hat,
Pretending it was cool and flat.
But gusts of wind blew past in haste,
Off it tumbled—what a waste!

Roots entwined, they made a band,
Playing tunes across the land.
Crickets danced, bugs brought the beat,
Join the party—feel the heat!

So when you wander on your way,
Hear the laughter, join the play.
Nature's stories, full of flair,
Bring a smile if you dare!

Ancient Arbor Anecdotes

There once was a tree, very tall,
Who thought itself the best of all.
A squirrel chuckled, took a seat,
Said, "Buddy, you can't always compete!"

The old oak claimed to touch the sky,
But lost a branch with a big goodbye.
Raccoons rolled with squeaky glee,
"Falling's silly—come climb with me!"

Cypress shared its wisdom deep,
"Don't be a tree that cannot leap!"
But knots just laughed at its decree,
"Branch out more—be kind, be free!"

The tales they share among the leaves,
Make echoes in the autumn eves.
So pass a smile to the tallest one,
The forest's fables can be such fun!

Lullabies of the Laburnum

Golden blooms in breezy sway,
Swaying softly, come what may.
Bumblebees buzz sleepy tunes,
While frogs croon under bright moons.

A rabbit hops, dreaming of pie,
With visions of carrots stacked high.
Crickets chirp a lullaby song,
Guiding the sleepy all night long.

Whispers of wind kiss each leaf,
Making nature's dreams, oh so brief.
Hooting owls join the choir,
As sleepy minds drift and retire.

So lay back beneath the stars,
Join the magic, forget your scars.
The laburnum sings in the night,
A cozy end, everything's right!

Chronicles of the Cedar

In the woods where whispers grow,
Cedars chuckle, putting on a show.
Squirrels gossip, they can't be beat,
Dance to the rhythm of tiny feet.

Bark and branches tell a joke,
As the sunlight starts to poke.
Frogs on logs are in on it too,
Ribbiting secrets, who knew it could brew?

Wind carries the laughter high,
Leaves giggle, waving goodbye.
Trees nod, they all agree,
Life's a jest in their jubilee.

So gather round, hear the cheer,
Nature's punchlines, crystal clear.
In every rustle, a playful tease,
Cedar sagas, sure to please!

Stories in the Stump

On an old stump, tales unfold,
Of critters bold, and mischief told.
A badger dressed in a flowered gown,
Tripped on roots and tumbled down.

Raccoons rumble in midnight feasts,
With acorns turned into tasty treats.
Squirrels dart with a nutty flair,
Spreading laughter in the chill night air.

The wind chimes in, a snicker or two,
As branches tease the froxcocks' crew.
Each ring a laugh, a whispered jest,
In the heart of the forest, they're all impressed.

So listen close to the old stump's song,
Where stories of folly and fun belong.
Nature's comedy, ever so grand,
In this whimsical woodland land!

The Heartwood's Secret

The heartwood hides a tale untold,
Of lively shenanigans, brave and bold.
Between the rings, mischief brews,
With giddy laughter, the woodwork wooed.

A raccoon in pajamas, oh what a sight,
Hosting a party under the moonlight.
Chipmunks in tuxes, ready to groove,
As the trees sway, they all approve.

Knots in the wood chuckle and sway,
Echoes of humor fill up the day.
The sapling spins in a playful jest,
"Catch me if you can!" it squeaks, impressed.

So come take a peek at this merry show,
Where the heart of the forest puts on a glow.
With every chuckle, every smirk,
It's a secret kept where the critters lurk!

Murmurs of the Maple

Maples murmur in a sassy tone,
Sharing the tales of the woodland throne.
With syrupy smiles and branches bent low,
They giggle about the last winter's snow.

A woodpecker tap dances on a trunk,
While a hare pulls pranks, oh what a funk!
Leaves rustle, sharing their glee,
Nature's own comedy spree.

Beneath the boughs, a hedgehog sleeps,
Snuggled in laughter, the secret he keeps.
Ants on a journey with plans in their heads,
Carrying snippets of humor in threads.

When the sun dips low, the night takes flight,
Maples chuckle in the soft twilight.
In every whisper, a echo of fun,
A playful twist for everyone!

Twilight Tails of Trees

In the twilight glow, the trees start to giggle,
Branches sway lightly, as if they're doing a wiggle.
Squirrels in suits throw a party with flair,
While the owls hoot tunes, floating fresh air.

The moon bounces in, with a smile on its face,
Sharing cookies with raccoons, what a wild chase!
Leaves whisper secrets, like gossiping friends,
As fireflies dance, and the laughter extends.

A deer cracks a joke, it's a real hoot,
A porcupine snickers, shaking its boot.
The night is alive, with laughter and cheer,
In the forest of fun, it's the best time of year.

As dawn softly breaks, the giggles will fade,
The trees hold their secrets, in shadows well laid.
But come night again, they'll return for the show,
Where squirrels in suits steal the scene with a bow.

Dreams Beneath the Dripline

Beneath the dripline, where raindrops play,
The critters convene at the end of the day.
A frog in a top hat sings songs from the bog,
While snails in a conga line hop like a dog.

The puddles reflect, all the silliness bright,
As ants run a race, giving it all in delight.
A turtle reports on the gossiping breeze,
Saying, "Did you hear? The crows made a tease!"

Ladybugs join in, checking fashion in style,
While a wise old owl watches all with a smile.
"Take life as it comes," says a wise little bee,
"Just dance in the rain, let your spirit be free!"

As the stars peek out, the chatter will pause,
Yet dreams will continue, without any cause.
For deep in the forest, where laughter aligns,
A party waits nightly, with dreams 'neath the pines.

The Forest's Chronicle of Time

In the forest's embrace, time dances away,
With trees leaning in for a curious play.
A chipmunk turns pages of tales that are tall,
While squirrels spread rumors from summer to fall.

The pines tell stories of snowflakes and sun,
Of critters who laugh, and of races they run.
With whispers of wind, and rustling leaves,
The forest rejoices as everyone weaves.

A hedgehog recites all the myths of the night,
While crickets compose music that feels just right.
"Did you see that?" yells a partridge with glee,
"I swear that I saw an owl dancing free!"

As the sun dips low and the twilight awakes,
The forest holds secrets, like delicious cakes.
Each creature a character in nature's own rhyme,
Forever they'll frolic, in the chronicle of time.

The Woodland's Whims

In the woods where shadows play,
Squirrels plot their grand buffet.
Acorns chime with a nutty joke,
As branchy friends begin to poke.

Bunny hops with a cheeky wink,
Sipping dew from a tiny drink.
The trees lean in, they want to hear,
The tales of mischief, laughter, cheer.

A raccoon dons a hat askew,
Declaring, "I'm the king! Who knew?"
Feathers fly from a playful crow,
While snakes tell tales of their cool, slow flow.

In this kingdom of giggles and glee,
Every leaf holds a secret decree.
Nature's jesters, loud and spry,
In the woodland's whim, we laugh and sigh.

Stories in the Soil

Down below where the critters scurry,
Worms weave tales without a hurry.
Stones and roots, they nod in glee,
Revealing secrets of what used to be.

A tiny beetle spins a yarn,
Of distant lands and a grand barn.
While ants declare their food regime,
Fighting over crumbs like it's their dream.

The roots whisper of storms long gone,
In rich soil, they sing their song.
Fungi giggle as they creep,
Unraveling stories, buried deep.

In this earthy, wondrous place,
Each grain holds a tale, a trace.
A mosaic of chuckles lies beneath,
In whispers, laughter, and a bit of teeth.

Sentinels of Story

Old trees stand, their arms stretched wide,
Guardians of tales that never hide.
With bark that cracks and leaves that sway,
They hold the laughter of the day.

The owls hoot, spinning riddles bright,
Under the moon's soft, silvery light.
The wind carries secrets, a gentle swoop,
While foxes share their nighttime scoop.

Each branch offers a comfy seat,
For woodland critters who love to meet.
Gathered 'round with twinkling eyes,
They swap their antics and silly lies.

Storytellers, both bold and spry,
Lift spirits up into the sky.
With every giggle and joyous cheer,
The sentinels of story stand ever near.

The Acorn's Account

Little acorn, snug on the ground,
Dreams of growing tall and round.
"One day I'll be a mighty tree!"
It squeaks with a hopeful glee.

But nearby, the bunnies hop,
Chasing tails, they never stop.
"Oh dear acorn, don't lose your way,
Join us, join us, come out and play!"

The frogs croak with boisterous pride,
"You'll miss the fun if you hide!"
With a giggle, the acorn grins,
"I'll sprout my roots, let the games begin!"

And so it dreams, as days go by,
In whispers of wind, it lifts its eye.
For every laugh and every cheer,
The acorn knows it will soon appear.

The Timbered Voice

In the woods where the squirrels play,
Trees gossip in their own quirky way.
They whisper secrets, they share a laugh,
Creating tales of a leafy gaffe.

A crow caws loudly, trying to sing,
While branches sway, doing their thing.
'Did you hear about the spruce on the hill?'
'Oh do enlighten, it's a tale to thrill!'

Beneath the bark, the rumor grows,
Of acorns lost and an owl's woes.
Each knot and ring holds a punchline bright,
As laughter echoes through day and night.

They chat away, these trees so wise,
In their own world, under sunny skies.
With every breeze, their chuckles rise,
Nature's jesters, the leafy guys.

Sylvan Stories Unveiled

In the thicket, a billy goat grins,
He's heard tales of the hare's silly wins.
A raccoon chuckles, a fox runs by,
'Did you see the owl? He tried to fly!'

The pines all giggle when deer prance around,
Each misstep leads to a silly sound.
'Oh dear,' says one, with a bark of glee,
'They tripped on roots, and now they flee!'

A weasel whispers, with a twinkling eye,
'Last week, I saw the fawn try to lie!
He claimed he'd seen a snake dance with glee,
But all he caught was a bumble bee!'

Underneath the moon, the forest sways,
With playful tales of fantastical days.
Each trunk bears witness, each leaf a friend,
Spinning stories that'll never end.

Murmurs of the Majestic Pines

Among the pines, where the breezes tease,
The trees tell stories with rustling ease.
They speak of a squirrel who fell from grace,
After chasing a nut in a crazy race.

The owls hoot softly, sharing a jest,
'You'd think that bird could fly with the best!'
As branches respond with an airy cheer,
'Remember the crow? He lost his gear!'

A chorus of laughter, the wind joins in,
Echoing the tales where fools begin.
'Oh squirrel,' they giggle, 'what a faux pas!
You danced with shadows and tripped on a straw!'

As twilight settles, their whispers fade,
But the humor lingers, in every glade.
With smiles in the bark and glee in the leaves,
Nature's mirth is one that never leaves.

Nature's Silent Narratives

In the glen where the green things grow,
Stories entwine in a humorous flow.
A raccoon once claimed he could outsmart,
A sleepy old turtle, but bless his heart!

The beetles debate on their shiny shells,
Spinning tales of the snails' fancy spells.
'Did you see them dance, oh what a sight?
Just sliding along, trying to look light!'

With every gust, the leaves conspire,
Sharing winks and giggles, stirring up fire.
The crickets chirp in a comical band,
As nature laughs at her own grand stand.

Beneath the stars, secrets are shared,
Of mishaps and mix-ups, no one prepared.
In the heart of the woods, the stories unfold,
Crafted in laughter, a treasure untold.

The Leaf's Legacy

In the breeze, a leaf took flight,
Twirling round in sheer delight.
A squirrel chuckled, 'What a show!'
As it danced to earth, a grand finale below.

The leaf proclaimed, 'I've tales to tell!'
Of acorns, ants, and a clear, blue well.
With a giggle, the critters took a seat,
For a storytime moment, oh, what a treat!

As the sun began to set low,
The leaf grew wise with every glow.
It bumbled on with tales of jest,
Leaving all the critters truly impressed!

And when the night came, they had a feast,
Of nuts and berries, celebrations increased.
The leaf grinned wide, happy and free,
In the heart of the glade, such glee it would see.

Chronicle of the Charmed Glade

In a glade where laughter bloomed,
The flowers chatted, never assumed.
'Do you hear the owl in the tree?'
'He hoots like he's in a comedy spree!'

A chipmunk paused, snacks in his paws,
'Who'd win in a race? The tortoise or applause?'
'The tortoise, no doubt, has the smarts!'
While the rabbits rolled on, each one with their carts.

They summoned the frogs for a talent show,
With croaks and plops, they brought quite the flow.
'With these tunes, we could start a band!'
Claimed a little firefly upon the stand.

Beneath the moon, the giggles awoke,
The trees whispered tales, even they cracked a joke.
In the charmed glade, where the wild things play,
Laughter's the currency, brightening the day.

The Dialogue of the Dappled

The dappled light felt quite mischievous,
Chattering softly, oh, how frivolous!
'Have you seen that crow strut around?'
'He thinks he's the king; so proud, so profound!'

In this playful patch of glimmer and shade,
The ferns chimed in, their tune never delayed.
'A squirrel stole my berry; I'm feeling quite blue!'
'You should dress like him! A nutty costume will do!'

The sunlight giggled, casting a grin,
'With costumes and capers, let the fun begin!'
And shadows gave whispers, light-hearted and sly,
'We'll make this a party! Oh my, oh my!'

In joyous delight, they all twirled and spun,
The dappled daylight, how it had fun!
With antics and pranks, the whole glade aglow,
In this whispered delight, the laughter would flow.

Whispers in the Underbrush

In the underbrush, whispers did thrive,
As critters conspired, so cunning, alive.
A tortoise declared, 'Let's start a race!'
'But I'll need snacks for my slow, steady pace!'

A bushy-tailed fox with a sly little grin,
Said, 'Join me, shall we? I promise to win!'
'But wait!' hollered a rabbit with a bounce,
'Let's place some bets, let's see who'll denounce!'

They set a stage made of twigs and some leaves,
For tales of old and for giggles, believes.
The underbrush buzzed, with laughter and cheers,
As friendships were forged, dissolving all fears.

And when the moon rose, their stories rang clear,
Of races and banter, they all held dear.
In the underbrush, where secrets confide,
Whispers of joy would forever abide.

The Forest's Confession

In whispers of the pine, secrets they share,
The squirrels plan a coup—quite the wild affair.
Mice in tiny suits plot midnight feasts,
While owls roll their eyes, calling them beasts.

The beavers are busy, building a dam,
Grinning with pride at their engineering jam.
Rabbits hold court at the foot of a tree,
Deciding the fate of a runaway pea.

A bear called Fred thinks he's quite the star,
Stealing the show from a raccoon with a scar.
The trees try to giggle, but it's quite hard,
When wiggles of laughter come from their yard.

Underneath their bark, truth goes around,
Hilarity reigns where no one is bound.
With giggles and grumbles, they're mighty fine,
Living in humor, like grapes on a vine.

Beneath the Bark

Beneath the bark, the critters conspire,
To outdo each other in tales of wild fire.
The ants think they're giants, none can dispute,
While toads sing along in their croaky pursuit.

A fox tells a tale of a brave hunter's chase,
While the skunks roll their eyes, knowing their place.
The porcupines poke fun at the quail's clumsiness,
As laughter erupts, spreading joy and fun-ness.

A chipmunk declares it's his birthday today,
He invites all the forest to party and play.
But the owls just hoot, with a wink and a nod,
Remarking on how this nutball is odd.

So gather 'round friends, hear their stories light,
Under the moon, in the cool of the night.
With jokes and with jests, the forest alive,
In a world full of laughter, we all can thrive.

Tales from the Canopy

From high in the branches, the parakeets cheer,
Chattering stories, all filled with good cheer.
The woodpeckers drum to a silly old tune,
While the bats play poker beneath the big moon.

A sloth brings a snack, oh, how slow he creeps,
While busy raccoons don their night-time keeps.
The leaves start to giggle at the funny display,
As ole' Badger waltzes, like he's on Broadway.

The branches sway gently, holding all the glee,
As butterflies flutter with spontaneous esprit.
The sky's painted pink, like a marshmallow treat,
While squirrels tell riddles that can't be beat.

A chorus of laughter fills the forest high,
As stories unravel beneath the cool sky.
In the heart of the woods, mischief takes flight,
Creating memories that shine in the night.

The Language of Leaves

In the breeze, the leaves share gossip untold,
Whispering secrets that never get old.
A maple snickers at a birch's new hat,
As the oaks roll their eyes, saying, "Fancy that!"

A dandelion laughs, "I'm a weed but so bright!"
"Don't worry," sighs moss, "it's all part of the sight."
The pine needles chuckle, "The more, the more fun!"
While acorns make bets on who'll be the next bun.

Through rustling and chuckling, they sway in delight,
Filling the air with their playful insight.
"Let's play hide and seek!" cries a willow with glee,
While the ferns play it cool and sip their sweet tea.

So if you find your way to the green of the trees,
Listen close to the laughter on each gentle breeze.
For nature's own humor is a joy to observe,
In the language of leaves, there's laughter to serve.

Chronicles of the Crosscut

In the woods where chainsaws sing,
A squirrel stole my coffee ring.
The trees laughed in leafy delight,
As I searched for my brew in the fading light.

A woodpecker danced, drumming his beat,
While I tripped over roots, oh what a feat!
The logs rolled by, in a game of charades,
While the moon chuckled, hiding in shades.

Branches whispered their tall tales,
Of critters and mischief, like ships with sails.
As I stumbled through underbrush thick,
Nature giggled at my old hiking trick.

So if you wander where trees intertwine,
Prepare for laughter and moments divine.
Just remember to watch your step next time,
Or join the forest's silly rhyme.

The Heart of the Heartwood

In the depths of the forest, a secret is kept,
Where laughter of logs leaves the meek quite inept.
A tree tried to tickle a lumberjack's nose,
And the bark rolled its eyes as the prank quickly rose.

The beavers held meetings; they plotted with glee,
To build dams that looked like a great big marquee.
While the owls in their wisdom, blinked down in awe,
At the chaos and fun that they saw in the raw.

A chipmunk collected what snacks he could find,
Though ants took his treasures and said, "You're so blind!"
So in this odd circus of branches and rays,
You'll giggle through woods on the silliest days.

Echoes of laughter, a whimsical breeze,
Nature's odd drama can put you at ease.
Step lightly, watch closely, and you just may see,
The heartwood of humor in every tall tree!

Echoes in the Hollow

In the hollow, a raccoon wore a hat,
As he danced with a lizard who fancied a spat.
They juggled acorns, oh what a sight,
While the frogs held a concert till late in the night.

The owls hooted their wise old tunes,
As fireflies twinkled like soft little moons.
A beech tree giggled, leaning too far,
And whispered to me, "Life's a strange bazaar!"

The moose had a party, the deer on the side,
Claimed they'd been invited, but slept when they tried.
While the wind played a melody, wild and free,
In the hollow, each echo was silliness' key.

So if you wander beneath shadow and glint,
Listen closely—oh, what a hint!
Of the laughter that pulses through leaves and old logs,
As night wraps the forest in giggles among frogs.

Sylvan Secrets Revealed

In the glen, where shadows prance,
A hedgehog taught a porcupine to dance.
With twirls and spins so comical to see,
The turtles cheered, saying, "Follow me!"

A pine tree sighed, its branches so low,
As squirrels rehearsed for the woodland show.
With acorns as popcorn and leaves as a stage,
The critters all laughed—nature's bright page.

The rabbits held court in their thicket of green,
Declaring the funniest creature in scene.
As the sun started setting, their giggles took flight,
Bringing joy and pure fun to the still of the night.

So heed these secrets that plant life will tell,
In the whimsical woods where all creatures dwell.
For laughter's a treasure that blooms with each beat,
In the heart of the forest, where life feels complete.

Glimmering in the Glade

In the woods where the critters dance,
A squirrel steals a snack at a glance.
With acorns piled high in a tree,
He giggles and chirps, oh, so carefree.

The rabbits play hopscotch in bloom,
While owls play poker in the dusk's loom.
A bear juggles pinecones with flair,
As laughter echoes through cool, crisp air.

Woodpeckers bob to a rhythm divine,
While the frogs croak their own silly line.
In this gleeful gathering we find,
Nature's humor, warm and kind.

Nestled in nature, joys collide,
With each little jest that the forest denied.
So giggle and guffaw in this glade,
Where the wild and the wacky invade!

Voices of the Verdant

In the heart of the shrubs where secrets reside,
A snail sings a tune that he can't quite abide.
With each note he slimes, a path is unfurled,
The mushrooms all chuckle—oh, what a world!

The badgers pull pranks while the hedgehogs conspire,
To smear all the trees with green goo that's flyer.
A chatty chipmunk, full of delight,
Tells tales of the moon's stolen light.

The crickets provide a comedic serenade,
As the fireflies flash a light masquerade.
In this leafy landscape alive with mirth,
The sounds of the forest bring giggles to birth.

So gather 'round, friends, let your laughs intertwine,
In a joyful cacophony—oh, how divine!
These voices of green, so happy and bright,
Remind us of laughter under the starlight.

Cedars and Secrets

Under the shade of the tall cedar trees,
The raccoons are plotting their next little tease.
With masks on their faces and paws in a bind,
They giggle and chuckle, no care left behind.

The squirrels whisper stories of mischief and fame,
As the pine cones roll in their humorous game.
With a hop and a skip, they draw in a crowd,
While owls just hoot, feeling wise and so proud.

The deer, quite bemused, just stare in surprise,
As the antics unfold right before their wise eyes.
What a sight to behold in the dense, leafy net,
Where the cedars and secrets are so hard to forget.

So dance with the shadows, and laugh till you fall,
In this whimsical world that enchants one and all.
With stories of old, carried on the breeze,
Cedars hold magic that brings us to our knees!

Whispers of the Willow

Beneath the willow, where the branches sway,
A frog croaks a tune that makes the bugs play.
With splashes of laughter in the rippling brook,
Nature composes a whimsical book.

Each leaf rustles soft tales of the day,
As a hen joins in for a comedic ballet.
With each quack and chirp, the pond comes alive,
As the insects buzz by, they cheer and they dive.

The sun casts a glow on the light-hearted scene,
As bunnies bounce by, all fluffy and keen.
They whisper of pranks, of games that they've spun,
On this rosy, ridiculous day full of fun.

So come spin a yarn, where the giggles run free,
In the whispers of willows—a joyful decree.
With nature's own laughter, let merriment swell,
In this playful haven, all is well!

The Storyteller's Trunk

In a trunk, big tales reside,
Wooden whispers never tried.
Squirrels gossip, owls wink,
Nature's tales, in wood, we think.

The raccoon's quest for tasty snacks,
Caught in a twig's sneaky traps.
A chipmunk's dance, a fox's prance,
Under the sun's warm, bouncy glance.

Bark is thick, but stories thin,
Tall tales grow as we check in.
Acorns fall with a little plop,
Echoing giggles, flop after flop.

So gather round, let's share a jest,
In the trunk, humor's at its best.
Nature's laughter won't be still,
In the woods, let's get our fill.

Beneath the Branches

Under branches, secrets swirl,
Where nature gives a merry twirl.
The ants march in a parade line,
Working hard, but oh, so fine!

A squirrel snickers, tail in tow,
As two birds bicker in the show.
Who gets the worm, who takes the seed?
Beneath the branches, oh, what greed!

With little feet, the owls convene,
Planning pranks that stay unseen.
They hoot with glee, share silly jokes,
Making mischief with the other folks.

Each leaf a witness to the fun,
While rays of sun make shadows run.
So grab some laughs, and take a peek,
Beneath the branches, joy's mystique.

The Canopy's Chronicles

In the canopy, stories writ,
Wooden records, never quit.
A woodpecker drums a silly beat,
As the sun gets up from its sleep.

Frogs croak secrets, in a choir,
To the beetles, who never tire.
The sunbeams flash, in twinkling ways,
Tickling leaves through the warm days.

When the breeze lifts and sways the trees,
Laughter floats like a gentle tease.
A butterfly flits, wearing a hat,
While raccoons plot, do you hear that?

Up high where pranks are free to soar,
The stories gather, forever more.
So climb aboard, let's disappear,
In the canopy, joy is near.

Nature's Newsprint

On nature's page, stories dictate,
Tall tales spin, we celebrate.
Each rustling leaf shares a scoop,
Tales of critters, in their loop.

The hedgehog writes with prickly style,
The news is hot, stick around a while.
The doves deliver, a paper plane,
Hooray for gossip, it's not in vain!

Raccoons in masks steal the show,
With headlines that are high, not low.
The rabbit hops in with a grin,
Nature's newsprint, let tales begin!

So read along with chirps and croaks,
Find joy within the fun, no hoax.
Nature's laughter paints the ink,
In every tale, we share and link.

The Gnarled Memoirs

Once there was a squirrel so sly,
He thought that he'd give flying a try.
He jumped from a branch,
And straight fell with a crunch!

The oak laughed loud, it was hard not to chuckle,
While the pine kept a grin, though it tried not to buckle.
The saplings just swayed,
Unaware of the charade.

One day a worm dared to climb up a tree,
Claiming he'd soon reach the sky, just wait and see!
But he wriggled and squirmed,
And his plans quickly germed.

So the forest, it chuckles with tales so absurd,
Of critters with dreams that were never deferred.
They twist and they weave,
In the woods, no reprieve.

Betrayals in the Underbrush

The raccoon stole snacks, oh what a delight,
While the owl just observed, keeping watch at night.
When dawn broke, he'd gloat,
'The thieves have no hope!'

A snail got too bold, decided to race,
While the tortoise chuckled, just slow at his pace.
'I'll win!' said the snail,
'Though my trail's like a fail!'

Behind leaves, two chipmunks plotted with glee,
To scare off a cat, oh, what a sight to see!
But the cat just yawned,
And their plans were all pawned.

They gathered their tales, each story a blast,
Each creature had secrets from first to the last.
In the thicket of fun,
Their mischief's begun.

Woodland Whispers

In the thicket, a rabbit did hop,
With a fumble and tumble, he couldn't quite stop.
He crashed through some ferns,
With a chorus of churns.

A hedgehog nearby quietly sneered,
'You call that a jump? I've truly no fear!'
But he rolled down the hill,
With a bump and a thrill.

At dusk, the fireflies started to glow,
While a curious fox put on quite a show.
He danced in the light,
And gave all a fright!

The woods echoed laughter, both near and afar,
As critters played pranks beneath the evening star.
In shadows they'd scheme,
And plot in a dream.

Dialogues of the Dappled Light

Beneath the sun's rays, two squirrels did chat,
'Have you seen my stash? I lost it, what of that?'
With a chuckle, he said,
'It's under the shed!'

A busy little ant marched, all in a swirl,
He claimed he'd found treasure, oh magic in pearl!
But it was merely a crumb,
Yet he'd dance and he'd hum.

'What's that in the bushes?' whispered a hare,
'The bushy-tailed thief looks quite full of flair!'
Yet the thief turned to sneeze,
Oh, where is the peace?

In the dappled light, stories twist and contort,
Where laughter brings joy, it's never too short.
And each furry friend,
Knows fun has no end.

Whispers of the Woodland

In the woods where squirrels chatter,
Mice plot mischief, tails a-flatter.
A bat swings low, he's lost his way,
Mixing up night with the light of day.

Old owls hoot with a wink and grin,
Telling tales of the folks they've seen.
Frogs critique the frogs who croak,
Singing songs of the evening smoke.

Bunnies bounce and dogs just stare,
One sneaky fox tips his hat with flair.
Fawns giggle at the jesters' play,
As the trees stretch wide in their own ballet.

Secrets Beneath the Bark

Under bark where beetles sneak,
Life unfolds in a funny tweak.
Ants hold court, a tiny parade,
Discussing plans in their grand charade.

Mushrooms giggle as they grow,
Whispering secrets only they know.
Nuts drop down, with a plop and a thud,
Accusing squirrels of theft and mud.

A fox in tweed flaunts his swag,
Claiming that trees just brag and brag.
With every shake of the leafy crown,
Laughter echoes through the leafy town.

Echoes of the Ancient Grove

In the grove where wise ones wait,
Tree trunks gossip, that's their fate.
Raccoons swap stories 'til night is spent,
Of the sneaky snacks and where they went.

The old maple sways with a chuckle,
As critters gather for a huddle.
Foxy winks at the moonlit snare,
While crickets serenade love in the air.

A snail's slow dance draws quite the crowd,
While frogs ribbit, feeling so proud.
But the roots beneath just shake their heads,
At all the fuss above their beds.

Sapling Chronicles

Little sprouts with stories to tell,
Dream of heights and wish them well.
With each breeze they giggle and sway,
Fantasies of grandeur all day.

The tiniest acorns make their claim,
Vowing one day they'll find their fame.
Though they're small, they think it's prime,
Using humor to pass the time.

Worms whisper words of wisdom, too,
As raindrops catch the morning dew.
Saplings laugh at the older trees,
"Just wait and see, we'll get the breeze!"

The Oak's Old Lore

Oh Oak, you wise old tree,
What stories do you see?
The squirrels laugh, the branches sway,
In your shade, the kids at play.

You've seen the birds in flight,
And whispered secrets in the night.
With a creak and a groan, you stand so tall,
What tales you tell, oh, do share all!

Your bark's got wrinkles, wise and deep,
But watch your roots, don't fall asleep!
The wind will tell, the leaves will sing,
Of all the funny things spring can bring!

So, come and gather round your base,
We'll laugh together, a funny place.
For every ring holds laughter too,
Oh Oak, we love the tales from you!

Rustling Revelations

The leaves are gossiping high in the air,
Whispers of secrets, do you dare?
A rustle here, a quiver there,
What shenanigans could they share?

The breeze carries tales of the woodpecker's show,
And the dance of the raccoons in moonlight's glow.
With snickers and giggles, the branches unite,
To weave funny stories late into the night.

But oh, the birch thinks it's quite refined,
While the aspen blushes, too easily aligned.
Each rustle reveals a new funny plot,
Underneath the canopy, laughter's all we've got!

So, lift your ears to the trees and listen well,
For in their chatter, there's magic to tell.
In every leaf's flutter, a giggle hides,
Rustling reveals where humor resides!

Folklore of the Firs

In the shadow of the firs, wisdom roams,
Pine needles tickle, where laughter foams.
A squirrel spins yarns with a wink and a nod,
These evergreens dance, how funny they plod!

Tall tales of the forest, tall as the trees,
As critters unite in a moment of tease.
Who knew a pinecone could spark such delight,
Or that owls would chuckle at the moon's silly light?

With branches all waving, they join in the jest,
And laugh at the deer who thinks he's the best.
Firs know the gossip, hold it so dear,
In their boughs of laughter, we all gather near.

So pull up a log, let's giggle and chat,
Until fatigue sets in and we all tip our hat.
Fables of the firs, we'll treasure and know,
In every cackle and chuckle, laughter will flow!

Epistles from the Elders

The grand old trees, with branches so wide,
Write letters of laughter the forest's pride.
Each wrinkle a wisdom, each leaf a delight,
From acorn to canopy, the humor takes flight.

"Dear critters of mischief," the cedar begins,
"Remember to giggle as the daylight spins.
With roots howling tales and bark wearing a grin,
Life in the woods is a whimsical spin!"

"Cherish your moments and dance in the sun,
For the echoes of laughter are never outrun.
Pause for the humor in each passing breeze,
And celebrate joy, oh, do it with ease!"

So gather the letters, unroll every lore,
From ancient old trees, we're always wanting more.
For through every epistle, a chuckle appears,
As the elders of the woods tickle our ears!

www.ingramcontent.com/pod-product-compliance
Lightning Source LLC
Chambersburg PA
CBHW070751220426
43209CB00083B/819